heart lines

gemma troy

Andrews McMeel
PUBLISHING®

Andrews McMeel Publishing
a division of Andrews McMeel Universal
1130 Walnut Street, Kansas City, Missouri 64106

www.andrewsmcmeel.com

18 19 20 21 22 SHO 10 9 8 7 6 5 4 3 2

ISBN: 978-1-4494-9514-5

Library of Congress Control Number: 2018933832

Heart Lines was first published in Australia in 2018
by Affirm Press.

ATTENTION: SCHOOLS AND BUSINESSES
Andrews McMeel books are available at quantity discounts
with bulk purchase for educational, business, or sales
promotional use. For information, please e-mail the
Andrews McMeel Publishing Special Sales Department:
specialsales@amuniversal.com.

All of the backgrounds in these pages are photographs taken by Gemma at different times of day at her home on the Sunshine Coast. The differences in light and shadow represent the influence of nature on the page.

She has a heart line
deeper than most
from hands that are too soft
and eyes that are too kind
she collects feathers and shells
seed pods and anything else
she can't bear to leave behind
within these pages
you will find
the sun
the clouds
the rain
and the sky
you might also find
your own heart hidden
among these lines
where you once
couldn't find what you were looking for
but you are here now
I hope these words keep you warm
and that they are
all that you have been searching for

Gemma

If wishes do come true
I must have wished upon a star
because nothing on earth
compares to you

With change
comes the chance
to fall in love
with yourself again

How beautiful it is to be broken
and feel the healing your hands bring

I want to fall in love with myself
the way the night
falls in love with the moon

I'm upside down in love with you
or inside out
or outside in
whatever it is
you have my heart in a spin

Even with my eyes closed
you still look perfect to me

Some say I have a big heart
then why do I feel so small

I love with everything
even if I'm given nothing

Let's begin again
that's always the best part

I have given you every other day
today
I'm giving to myself

Getting lost in you
was the best adventure
I have ever had

I cannot look at a sunset
and not think of you

When I'm with you
I miss me

I only orbit the sun
to be with you

But water doesn't mix with fire
and I am both

I don't know how to love
other than with every part of me
I don't know how to break
other than with every part of me

How quickly day
can become night
and love
can become hate

Kiss me
it's been so long
since I have seen stars

There are feelings in me
that don't even have a name yet

My heart
will always
find a way
to be close to yours

Find someone
with a backbone
strong enough
to carry you both

I will wait for you
like a star
until I too burn out

I'm so brutally hard with myself
and so unquestionably soft
with everyone else

You are not invisible
you are so rare
that not everyone
can see you

You can tell me goodbye
a thousand times
but I will only ever
remember your hello

She feels invisible
but she doesn't know
her light is blinding

I would walk through fire
again and again
if you were the prize
at the end

I don't want a forever with you
I just want you
here and now

I have tried crying you out
but there is an ocean of
you in me

My heart is fearless
and herein lies my problem

If I took these feelings I have for you
and stretched them out
they would wrap around the world
a thousand times

I love hard
and I break
just as hard
as I love

You are under my skin
each layer
a bed for you

I'm too much soul
and not enough body

She mapped out the features of his face
so she wouldn't forget the way back home

Sometimes it feels like
there are planets between us
but we are so stuck
in each other's gravity
I can feel the pull
toward you regardless

Whatever makes you feel the sun
from the inside out
chase that

If only my loneliness
would fall in love
with my solitude

If I loved you
any more fiercely
you might mistake me
for the sun

If hurting means that I have loved
then I hope
I will always feel pain

Soft hearts create
the most beautiful art

In your strength
I found mine

If love is the answer
I want to always
be the question

I hadn't tasted love
until I tasted you

After all is said and done
you will always be my favorite part

I'm lying at the bottom with you
and all I want to do is fall again

If only you knew
what your touch does to me
your hands
would never leave my body

I will let you hate me
if that's easier
than loving me

I guess I have myself to blame
I craved a love so deep
I didn't think about the consequences

I loved the stars
well before I knew
they were only beautiful
because of the dark

You crawled into my heart
fell asleep in there
and I have been dreaming of you
ever since

If I had to choose only one sense
it would be touch
for I crave your hands
more than anything

If I miss you any harder
my heart
might come looking for you

You make me smile
god you make me smile
the teeth-showing kind of smile
that stretches to the corners of my eyelids
until my eyes smile also

You smell like the sea
and the sea always smells like home

If I can survive the war
that I battle with myself
I can survive anything

Now that I know who you are
I miss the person
who I thought you were

I need to stop searching
for my heartbeat
in others

If anything
pain has made me strong
while love
has made me weak

I just want you
to want the pieces of me
that you cannot see

It's terrifying
how deep my heart
is willing to love you
without fear

Out of all the people
I miss right now
I miss myself the most

I never want to be okay without you
I never want us to end
I never want to be the heartbreak
that my poetry penned

In the act of falling
I learned the skill of flying
and in the art of breaking
I learned the magic of healing

Find a tender heart
and be prepared
for a lifetime
of love

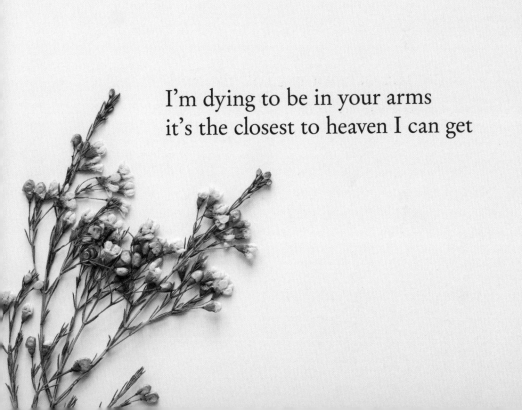

I'm dying to be in your arms
it's the closest to heaven I can get

Like the ocean on a full moon
I'm drawn to you

Your touch ignites
forest fires
across my skin

She was the gravity
that held the earth
firmly in place

My heart is so full of you
you are spilling over
into every part of me

Don't ever stop loving me
can you imagine
the earth without her sun

I refuse to be malleable
in anyone's hands
but my own

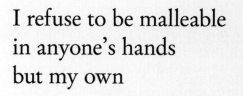

Today I am broken
but tomorrow I could
become someone's universe

I'm not sure if I want this anymore
but I am human
so I will endure it nonetheless

You hold happiness in your arms
that's why it's my favorite place to be

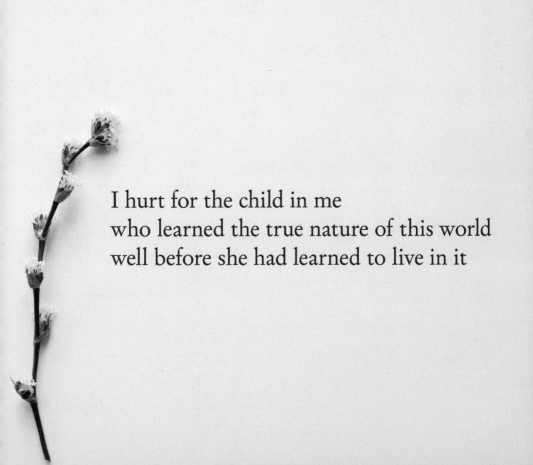

I hurt for the child in me
who learned the true nature of this world
well before she had learned to live in it

I often feel like a guest
in my own heart
since you moved in

I owe fate a thank-you
for giving me you

You make me feel seen

Tears are how you water your soul
so you can grow

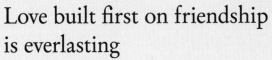
Love built first on friendship
is everlasting

Come back to me
the rain won't stop falling
and I'm so cold without the sun

I can't stop wanting you
just like I can't stop breathing

Sometimes we need
to be burned to the ground
to be able to begin again

You are the moon
I am the sun
you rise to light the dark
I burn to light the day

Your heart
is so soft with mine
it too knows
that falling stars
don't last in time

You are not here
and yet
there is no distance
between us

You are love
and I'm here
just trying to catch
a drop of it

You are summer
to my winter heart

The only secret I never told
was how much my heart
relied upon yours

For too long
I have been worried
about what others thought of me
when I should have been worried
about what I thought of myself

I would live a thousand lifetimes
just to meet you
in this one

Your love paints my heart gold

Maybe the stars fall
because it's the only way
we know how to share our light

Once a month
the pain in my heart
moves down to the pit of my stomach
and I'm reminded
of the universe that lies within

You have entered
my atmosphere
and I will forever
be breathing you in my dear

The air is thick
with everything I want to say
but will never have the courage to

Remember your words
can plant gardens
or burn
whole forests down

You bent the light in such a way
I fell in love
with every color that you made

Your touch
is pure sunshine

I'm not scared to hand myself over to you
I'm scared you won't hand anything back

I am afraid to show the real me
that I will be
too real for you
too hard for you
too much of everything for you
and never enough

I have tried loving less
but that hurts
just the same

My heart begins
at your fingertips

Does she know
the world beats inside her
and no matter how many times
you try to blind her
her sun rises every damn day

I'm in love with you
I know this
because
I can no longer feel my heartbeat
I can only feel yours

Her heart bloomed sunflowers
so she would always face the light

You are stuck in my lungs
I cannot breathe in
I cannot breathe out
is this what they call love

She has given so much of herself
that when alone
there is barely enough
to keep her breathing

How beautiful you bloom
when you nurture your roots

I fall in love with eyes
because they cannot hide
even the most cunning of lies
and yours my dear
are crystal clear
with the most beautiful shade of aqua blue
even if you are not here
the sky is my constant reminder of you

Your heart is the softest landing
I have had yet

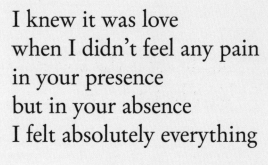

I knew it was love
when I didn't feel any pain
in your presence
but in your absence
I felt absolutely everything

I can either let
the missing you
drown me
or I can let it teach me
how to swim

There is the sun
and the earth
the moon and the stars
the clouds and the sky
and then there is you and I

Kiss the parts of my soul
that have turned dark
and bring me back to the light

She built walls for her own protection
only to be entombed within

Finding a pure heart
is like digging for gold

The capacity to hurt and love
at the same time
is what makes us human

I hope I made you feel something
because you made me feel everything

I miss you
in ways
that not even I
can understand

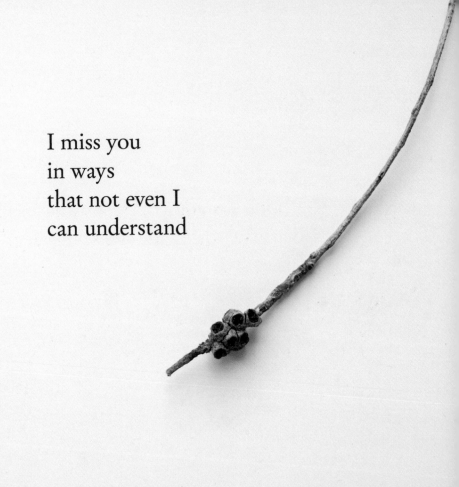

Don't love me in pieces
if you want me whole

I miss the way my heart
pools at your feet
when you touch me from within

I'm not responsible
for what my heart
wants to do

My favorite parts of you
are the ones you leave behind
on my lips
between my legs
within my heart
and on my mind

Today I miss you
a little more than yesterday

The moon woke me last night
it didn't want to miss the stars
like I have been missing you

I don't know how to unlove
so I will always love you

I want to live
where the clouds touch the sky
I'm told the love there
never dies

I'm going to love you
until
I'm no longer body
and only soul

How many times
will I burn
before I learn
self-love
doesn't involve a flame

If you don't get lost
once in a while
how do you ever expect
to find yourself

The path to my past
is so well worn
I can walk it
with my eyes closed

I would tear every limb
from my body
and offer them to the gods
in exchange for you

You have my heart
don't forget to feed it love
so it will keep beating

I want more of you
to want more of me

I'm missing you in months
even though it has only been seconds
since I have loved you in years

The world is so beautiful
stop looking for things
to cloud your vision

Our love isn't perfect
but it's ours